# MAC'S FIELD GUIDE™

## TO MOUNT RAINIER NATIONAL PARK

## WILD FLOWERS

ART BY CRAIG MACGOWAN, DAVID SAUSKOJUS, AND STEVEN WHITNEY

**Habitat**

M—meadows
W—woods
S—streams
WM—wet meadows
MW—moist woods
MA—marshes
R—dry, rocky places

**Bunchberry Dogwood**
*Cornus canadensis*
2"–8"; MW

**Vanilla Leaf**
*Achlys triphylla*
8"–16"; MW, S

**Trillium**
*Trillium ovatum*
4"–16"; W

**Marsh Marigold**
*Caltha biflora*
4"; MA

**Spring Beauty**
*Claytonia lanceolata*
2¾"–6"; M, W

**Western Pasqueflower**
*Anemone occidentalis*
4"–24"; WM, M

**Avalanche Lily**
*Erythronium montanum*
10"; WM

**Meadow Parsley**
*Ligusticum grayi*
8"–24"; W, M

**Pearly–Everlasting**
*Anaphalis margaritacea*
8"–36"; M

**Sitka Valerian**
*Valeriana sitchensis*
12"–48"; WM, MW

**Partridgefoot**
*Luetkea petinata*
2"–6"; MW

**Beargrass**
*Xerophyllum tenax*
24"–60"
W, M

**White Heather**
*Cassiope mertensiana*
12"; M

**Thinleaf Blueberry**
*Vaccinium membranaceum*
36"–120"; M

**Cascade Blueberry**
*Vaccinium deliciosum*
6"–12"; M

**Corn Lily**
*Veratrum viride*
36"–84"; WM, MA

**Mountain–Ash**
*Sorbus scopulina*
13'; WM

**Red Huckleberry**
*Vaccinium parvifolium*
36"–72"; W

**Black Alpine Sedge**
*Carex nigricans*
2"–14"; WM

**Tiger (Columbia) Lily**
*Lilium columbianum*
12"–48"; M, W

**Buttercup**
*Ranunculus eschscholtzii*
8"; R, WM

**Glacier Lily**
*Erythronium grandiflorum*
6"–12"; M

**Skunk Cabbage**
*Lysichitum americanum*
12"–36";
MA, S

**Coiled Beak Pedicularis**
*Pedicularis contorta*
8"–20"; M

**Bracted Pedicularis**
*Pedicularis bracteosa*
12"–36"; WM

**Cinquefoil**
*Potentilla spp.*
4"–14"; M

**Calypso Orchid**
*Calypso bulbosa*
2"–8"; MW

**Alpine Aster**
*Aster alpigenus*
2"–6"; M

**Fleabane (Mountain Daisy)**
*Erigeron peregrinus*
12"–30"; WM

**Lewis Monkeyflower**
*Mimulus lewisii*
12"–24"; WM, S

**Fireweed**
*Epilobium angustifolium*
36"–120"
MW, WM

**Spreading Phlox**
*Phlox diffusa*
4"–12"; R

**Sickletop Pedicularis**
*Pedicularis racemosa*
6"–20"; W

**Rosy Spirea**
*Spirea densiflora*
8"–40"; WM, R

**Cusick's Speedwell**
*Veronica cusickii*
2"–18"
WM, S

**Jeffrey Shooting Star**
*Dodacetheon jeffreyi*
24"; WM, S

**Elephanthead Pedicularis**
*Pedicularis groenlandica*
24"; WM

**Cliff Penstemon**
*Penstemon rupicola*
18"; R

**Magenta Paintbrush**
*Castilleja parviflora*
12"; M

**Red Columbine**
*Aquilegia formosa*
12"–36"; MW

**Red Heather**
Phyllodoce empetriformis
4"–16"; M

**Mountain Bog Gentian**
*Gentiana calcyosa*
2"–12"; WM, S

**Alpine Lupine**
*Lupines lepidus*
3"–4"; R

# MAC'S FIELD GUIDE™

## TO MOUNT RAINIER NATIONAL PARK

## TREES

**Key:** C—Cone; LVT—Leaflets; N—Needles; D—Diameter; LV—Leaves; R—Range; H—Height; L—Length; W—Width

**Vine Maple**
*Acer circinatum*
D 8"; H 25'
LV 2"–4" L x 2"–4" W
R 0'–5000'

**Bigleaf Maple**
*Acer macrophyllum*
D 3'–4'; H 30'–70'
LV 6"–10" L x 6"–10" W
R 0'–10,000'

**Douglas Maple**
*Acer glabrum*
H 25'
LV 1"–3" W x 2"–4" L
R 0'– 4000'

**Red Alder**
*Alnus rubra*
D 2'; H 50'–100'
LV 3"–5" L x 2"–3" W
R 0'–2500'

**Bitter Cherry**
*Prunus emarginata*
D 10"; H 60'
LV 1"–3"; R 900'–3000'

**Pacific Dogwood**
*Cornus nuttallii*
D 1'; H50'
LV 2.5"–4.5" L x 1"–2.5" W
R 0'–6000'

**Scouler Willow**
Salix scouleriana
D 1"–10"; H 3'–35'
LV 2"; R 0'–10,000'

**Pacific Crab Apple**
*Pyrus fusca*
D 8"–10"; H 30'
LV 2"–3" L; R 0'–1000'

**Western Red Cedar**
*Thuja plicata*
D 2'–8'; H 100'–175'
C 0.5"; R 0'–6000'

**Alaska Cedar**
*Chamaecyparis nootkatensis*
D 1'–4'; H 50'–100'; C 0.25"
R 0'–6000'

**Pacific Yew**
*Taxus revifolia*
D 2'; H 50'
N 0.75"; R 0'–7000'

**Subalpine Fir**
*Abies lasiocarpa*
D 1'–2.5'; H 50'–100'
C 2.5"–4"
N 1"–2"; R 4000'–8000'

**Pacific Silver Fir**
*Abies amabilis*
D 2'–4'; H 80'–150'; C 3"–6"
N 1.5"; R 0'–6000'

**Mountain Hemlock**
*Tsuga mertensiana*
D 1'–3'; H 30'–100'
C 1"–3"; R 0'–2000'

**Western Hemlock**
*Tsuga heterophylla*
D 3'–4'; H 100'–150'
C 1"; R 0'–1500'

**Sitka Spruce**
*Picea sitchensis*
D 8'; H 200'; C 2.5"–4"
N 1"; R 0'–3000' S

**Engelman Spruce**
*Picea engelmannii*
D 1.5'–2.5'; H 80'– 100'
C 1'–2"
N1"; R 2000'–10,000'

**Noble Fir**
*Abies procera*
D 2.5'–4'; H 100'–150';
C 4.5"–7"
N 1"; R 3000'–7000'

**Grand Fir**
*Abies grandis*
D 1'–3'; H 100'–200'
C 2"–4"
N 1"–2"; R 0'–9000'

**Douglas Fir**
*Pseudotsuga menziesii*
D 2'–5'; H 80'–200'
C 2"–3"
N 0.75"–1.25"; R 0'–6000'

**Whitebark Pine**
*Pinus albicaulis*
D 1'–2'; H 20'–50'
C 2"–6"
N 1.5"–2.75"
R 3500'–above

**Ponderosa Pine**
*Pinus pnderosa*
D 3'–4'; H 60'–130
C 2"–6"
N 5"–8"; R 1500'–4000'

**Lodgepole Pine**
*Pinus contorta*
D 1'–3'; H 20'–80'
C 1.5"–2"
N 2"; R 0'–9000'

**Western White Pine**
*Pinus monticola*
D 3'; H 100'; C 5"–9"
N 2"–4"; R 0'–6000'

978-0-89886-596-7 US $5.95


The Mountaineers, 1001 SW Klickitat Way, Suite 201, Seattle, WA 98134; (206) 223-6303
ISBN 0-89886-596-4

9 780898 865967